MAPPING A LIFE

MAPPING A LIFE

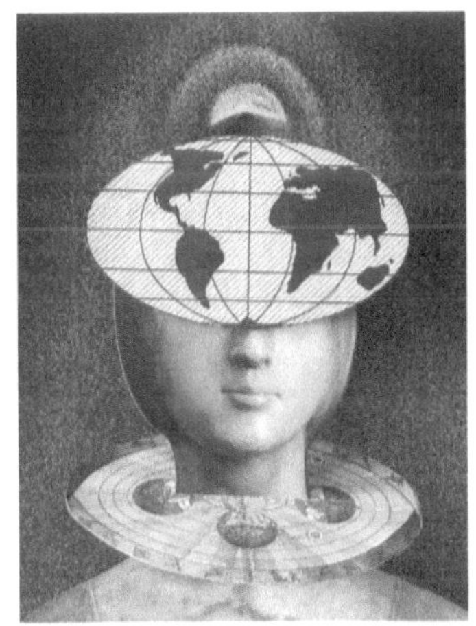

Poems by

Susan T. Moss

Antrim House
Bloomfield, Connecticut

Library of Congress Control Number: 2021917157

ISBN: 978-1-943826-92-6

First Edition, 2021

Printed & bound by Ingram Content Group

Book design by Rennie McQuilkin

Front cover photograph by Alexa Frangos

Author photograph by Hal Himmelstein

Antrim House
860.217.0023
AntrimHouseBooks@gmail.com
www.AntrimHouseBooks.com
400 Seabury Dr., #5196, Bloomfield, CT 06002

Acknowledgments

Grateful acknowledgment is made to the editors of the following publications where some of the poems in this volume previously appeared:

After Hours: "Ambiente," "Beach Time," "Broadway and Devon," "The Viewing"
Distilled Lives: "South Road"
in plein air: "Mapping A Life"
the Kerf: "No Ticket Required"
P2 Collective: "Beach Time," "Swimming Freestyle With My Mother," "Traveling the World"
Quill and Parchment: "Point of View"
Seeding the Snow: "Looking Down"
Soundings: Door County In Poetry: "Along the Way"
Steam Ticket: "Redwoods"
Winnetka Living: "Heading West"
Words Across the Water: "Katahdin," "Pinckneyville, August 21, 2017"

Thank you to members of the Illinois State Poetry Society, Poets Club of Chicago, the P2 Collective, Poets and Patrons, and participants of the Bjorklunden and The Clearing poetry workshops for their many insights and encouragement.

Also, thanks to family and friends who have supported my creative endeavors over the years. A special thank you to my editor and publisher, Rennie McQuilkin, for his astute suggestions and repartee. My deep gratitude, as always, goes to Hal Himmelstein for walking the path with me.

Table of Contents

I

II

MAPPING A LIFE

I

Mapping a Life

Sometimes it's like that: the kind
of journey when I walk
where deer prints mark a path
fringed with scallop-bottomed
mushrooms and speckled stones—
a microcosm of beauty and solitude
at each bend and in every breath
that reminds me I am not even
halfway to anywhere
with so much to examine, hold onto
before the urgency to repack
for life's next destination, another place
to meet myself at the still point.

Time's Landscape

This day, like all, holds much
to discover, inhale, store
for less lush times far
from folded mountains.

A post-breakfast walk
past Halloween scarecrows,
curious white chickens
and strutting roosters

to a covered bridge reveals a portrait
of distant village below
and tender mew and gurgle
of a stream purling toward the river,

its water pulsing each day
with its own rhythm and secrets,
every molecule joining this moment
already flowing downstream.

Later, while climbing the stairs
to my studio, I brush my hand
over a scented geranium—a lemon song
stroked into citrus melody.

Swimming Freestyle with My Mother

I finished the canned cling peaches
floating in pear juice you preferred
over heavy syrup.

The last sweet slices mingled
with other reminders
of our life together and apart,

each following her own current,
both swimming up stream
as age washed over you.

When the last of your pantry ran dry,
I waded through what my heart knows
of our shared laughter,

your wisdom and patience
that encouraged me to breathe
and stroke, kick and glide

in deep water and the shallows,
where it's just as easy to drown
if not alert to a sea change.

Redwoods

I am comfortable standing
among giants,
time's arboretum
higher than my reach
and wider than my grasp.
Their thousand years
of silence speak
relative eternity,
something beyond
what history easily
remembers
of sovereign relics
and survivors
of chop and hew.

Unless I leave the path
and step into the light,
the needled boughs
are hidden like Olympian gods
impervious to dancing
mayflies below.

Skyward

Even the tallest buildings
can't hide shafts of light
seeking canyon floors
now mostly deserted.

Sunshine strums windows
sandwiched between glow
and midpoint where bright
meets dusky depths

and leaves those of us
at virus ground zero
sheathed in masked hope
while tiptoeing

through the shadows
on a cloud-flecked day
with the only view
up.

Along the Way

The day is fine for early walking
in well-worn boots that leave
tracks on dawn-washed earth

baptized in spring light
and chastened by a loon's
mournful yodel from Ellison Bay's

rocky beach tumbled
with limestone shards,
chronicles of ancient life

below ridge-path surprise
of blue forget-me-nots, yellow
lady slippers and bits of fauna:

a butterfly wing still orange
and white inscribed with inky lines,
talisman of flight forever grounded;

a raccoon's skull not fully grown,
smudge of hair and cartilage—so little
left for nightly forages.

Mutable lifetimes transcribed in stone
and dust crumble and fade
like my footprints in the morning dew.

Late August

Green lawn gives way to patches
of brown and holes dug
by frenetic squirrels burying acorns
for their winter stash often lost
under piles of snow.

A stillness in the stately pines
and oaks contrasts with noisy
nibbling by these gray keepers
of this moment I observe
from a patio chair

while watching for other changes—
the instant when all meet
at the juncture of past
and future as an infinitesimal
thread connects us

with whatever went before and what
will follow, those things we can control
and those that pass us by;
courses through each leaf or disappears
when no one's left to remember.

Labyrinth

Five hundred candles blaze
a two-foot-wide path
toward the center distilled
from switchbacks and curves.

The infusion of light blooms
into a slow letting go
of night sounds and my clicking
heels on stone.

Consciousness untethers
its compass and like standing
on a galactic canopy, I roam
over the earth, look down

at wax stars or glowing souls
lifting me higher until no longer
weighted by the sins of the world,
backwash of hate or ghosts of self-pity.

Circling dissolves into my longing
to hold the instant where breath
and time eclipse what was and will be,
but I dare not linger

as the light starts to dim
along the journey
unwinding too quickly back
to where I started.

Cautious Optimism

I stand on the precipice
of memories evolving
into present wobbling
toward tomorrow.

I look left and see Santa Claus
perched on a passing firetruck;
above, a flock of sandhill cranes
migrating to the South

where meteors spackle
still, clear nights,
and sunny days
invite slow-motion living.

A half turn right reveals
paperwhites in winter bloom
and in the street a stray cat
calls to whoever will pet him.

Pivoting slightly to the southwest
I scan the sky for Saturn
and Jupiter snuggled together
after four hundred years.

It's important to watch
where I place my feet,
not knowing what lies ahead
while tucked between clarity

and shifting winds or sudden
earth tremors that could throw
off my balance and propel me
backward without a safety net.

Like a mountain climber
I tread lightly, keep my eyes
focused, hold on to caution
and don't get too close to the edge.

Point of View

We walk among the sea oats
swaying on lake breeze
while curling waves
unfold at shore's edge.

Gulls swoop and glide
in aerial outlook for fish
streaming below waterline
framed by cloudless horizon.

Here among transient grass
rooted to drifted sand,
apex sun drowns human failure
and unfulfilled dreams.

What abides with limited breath
will one day yield to earth but not
under Argus-eyed feet and our need
to bulletproof this beauty.

Secrets of Hawaii

In an underwater world open space
releases expectation, buoyancy
so different from sky-bound views
or gravity's pull.

We float and kick face down,
adjust our masks to view parades of fish—
black-banded yellow, iridescent blue
with orange spots, the occasional pink
or brown swimmers guided by tides'
ebb and flow, pursuing tiny nutrients
that cling to rocky ledges or coral reefs.

Sunning green turtles slip
from shore into ocean; swayed
and tumbled by waves, they swim
below us, oblivious to land-lovers
who begin to feel at home.

Where You Can Find Me

Yesterday we sat on the lighthouse lawn,
ate ice cream from a vendor's pushcart
and listened to band music with horns
blaring and timpani booming
while children tossed a plastic ball
that bounced off people's sandaled feet.

This morning's dark, August clouds
promised rain and threatened our swim
at the beach, but that didn't stop a dive
into lumpy waves before the sudden downpour
that sent us scuttling across wet sand
for cover under a stored canoe
where we sipped coffee from a blue thermos
and watched gulls fast-foot along the shore.

Later, mute sailboats traced the horizon
under clear skies as we walked over the dunes
and through another millimeter of time.
When you asked me where life was taking us,
I answered *here*.

II

Pinckneyville, August 21, 2017

We sit like hounds waiting
for the full moon after driving
three hundred miles to southern
Illinois under a periwinkle sky
to witness the demise
of glimmering sun louvered
by unchastened moon.
Its Goliath hold bends day
into dusk, brandishes winds
stopped in mid-leaf flutter
and taunts birds
into frenzied swoops.

On the courthouse square
no one speaks or notices
that traffic has stopped squeezing
like an accordion
past the locals and pilgrims
whose faces, slick with sun screen
and masked by cardboard solar glasses,
wait in the tarnished light.

Venus plays a cameo role as the moon,
wearing its radiant collar,
eclipses the sun while the speed
of now holds its breath.

Notes on Moscow

St. Basil's Cathedral, with blue,
green, red and yellow-striped onion
domes, watches over Red Square

and catches dawn's first blush in
late summer and like the Cathedral
of The Archangel, filled with icons

in muted palettes and brooding visages,
sheds its carnival lights competing
with GUM department store glitter

that attracts tourists and oligarchs
seeking Tiffany, Armani or the Gucci
fashion world contrasted with remnants

of the Soviet Union's hammer, sickle
and red stars replaced by the Russian flag.
This city of ambiguities holds tightly

to encrypted czars, czarinas' silver-
threaded ball gowns in golden palaces,
conquests, defeats and famine,

while cement block apartments slowly yield
to gleaming skyscrapers fingering
into the present. This weft and weave

of life includes crowded cafés and morning
barges in their routine passage on the
Moscow River under the Moskvoretsky

Bridge where dissident Boris Nemstov
was assassinated and still mourned
years later by many of the over twelve million

citizens who start their day waiting
for the proclaimed existential threats
while we all sleep with one eye open.

Great Wall of China

The stone structure twists
and turns through mountain
passes and over ridges—

a colossal effort that slices
the landscape, its barracks
and guard towers perched

above the fortress stretching
five hundred years
and thousands of miles,

with some sections now mounded
like sleeping camels given way
to time and decay

while outside Bejing, sunlight
glints off renovated granite steps
into the past.

All that effort to divide, repel
or impose, so much energy
to flaunt power and grandeur

beyond view—the age-worn
question of what we keep
walling in or walling out.

Ambiente

What I know of Spain is espadrilles,
tapas, rainbow-colored tiles, its
chronicles of civil war and religious
purges—a place where voices

curl upward from café chatter
toward my unshuttered window
and the ghosts of Cervantes, Lorca,
Jiménez whisper their poetry

under a full moon competing
with clacking bells from
hallowed churches on narrow
cobbled streets squeezed

between stone buildings
with hanging marigolds
and bird cages amid neatly
pinned laundry two floors above.

I also know of Miró's quest
for perfection with the fewest
brush strokes, Goya's
Black Paintings,

flamenco's clap, stomp and strum,
ripening oranges scenting
the Mezquita of Córdoba,
Barcelona's salt air

and seduction of rioja tinto sipped in
twelfth-century walled
cities like Hondarribia or Granada,
where the Alhambra looms

over the Albayzin, its dark rooms
weaving into more rooms with corners
of intrigue and hidden spaces,
inscrutable like my dreams.

Riding the Renfe Rails

Spain's countryside rushes
past the fast train from Madrid
to Sevilla.

Olive trees trace the contours
of hills, rolling up and over
the other side toward red clay

cotton fields, and tunnel's surprise
as landscape gently flattens
to a West Texas vista—

arid soil, grazing cattle, desolate
plains with prickly pear cacti
unlike the city with its cross-crested

spires that also dapple remote farmland
sprawling beyond castle ramparts
clinging to five hundred years

of decay while hulking wind turbines
spin above distant ridges absent
Don Quixote and Moorish Knights.

Random outcrops of orange-tiled
white casas layer texture to another
Andalucían portrait of Picasso

triangles, squares and grids
brush-stroked with trees dangling
little green fruit in this place

where time slows
and carries us like a river
beyond the distance

between beginning and end
where it's easier to float
when our feet don't scrape bottom.

Paddling the Zambezi

Common sense tells us not to do it.
The river opens wide to spanking waves
and uneven currents best left
to more expert canoeists.

But we have come thousands of miles
and driven over pocked roads
through mosquito-choked jungles.

When one last doubt takes flight
with an egret flapping over rippling water,
I settle in the bow where the less brawny
usually sits and navigate the next ten miles.

Hippos that stand knobby-knee deep
snort their warning not to come
between them and shore, make
dipping through murky water

less dangerous than veering
with the wind into these
glistening hulks and their calves.

Here Zimbabwean warthogs,
bulky-bodied with protruding snouts,
graze in the underbrush
and an African Fish Eagle shrieks
from a fan palm.

Riffles, white with churning, hook
our paddles, tug against reluctant muscles
needed later to maneuver unmarked shallows

grabbing the stern and threatening capsize.
Off shore two thin boys wait in a skiff
for small orange cichlids to swim their way.

Flecks of mud dry on my arms
grown comfortable with swinging
and stroking toward our campsite.
Rhythms of the river keep flowing through me.

Notes on La Tierra del Encanto

New Mexico's Sangre de Cristo Mountains
bleed amber, ochre, cinnabar and ivory tints
in high desert sun, their rainbow

silence hijacked by sporadic squawks
of black-billed magpies flapping over
sandstone mesas once seas now turned to dust.

Adobe houses with clay brick walls protrude
like fortresses among sage brush
and mesquite under unblemished skies.

Artists and Pueblo dwellers celebrate
what lies beyond backroads woven
among hills and scattered cattle—

a sunset burning iridescent pink and purple,
wild horses wandering over sacred land,
an expanse of forever.

Here shapes and colors speak in local
vernacular—howl with coyotes,
whisper from bleached bones

and dried red peppers, echo off
the Rio Grande gorge and sing
through the ponderosa pines.

Katahdin

The mountain bows
at its base and fans
into a trail narrowing
toward steep.

Short of a mile, pebbles
grow into boulders
arching through pine.

Cascading brook
blossoms and foams,
flashes under a bridge
far from taunting
summit above tree line

where toe by toe,
hand over hand,
rock-climbers cling
to edges along crevices
threatening the goal

of ridge beyond clouds,
hawks circling Maine woods
seeded with pocket-size ponds.

Blinks of humanity
goat foot past millions
of granite years
to stand on time's brow.

Kilauea

On the Big Island,
the earth spills its guts—
black molten bile creeps
down the streets,
blankets cars,
gorges on trees,
spits fire and smothers
the air with billowing smoke.

All the prayers to Pele,
the fire goddess, can't appease
her wrath flowing like tears.

With time new earth rebirths
as home to palms, hibiscus,
crimson-feathered apapane
and much aloha.

Rush

Once I decided
my tandem jump
partner didn't want
to die on an autumn
New Zealand day,

I didn't fear
our somersault roll
from a Cessna
at fifteen thousand feet
above white-mantled
mountains, bird flight
and sixty-second freefall

into silence with no earthly
means to measure
downward speed
or tangible borders

before pull of ripcord
and jerk of uplift
from open parachute's
catch of draft, surge
and riding the wind,

floating through
a cloudless sea
until horizon and barren
fields rose to meet us.

We took two steps forward
for a perfect landing
as tightened lines
grounded us—
a concept highly overrated.

Battle Harbor

An island grounded
on granite nine miles
off the Labrador coast hosts
white and yellow frame cottages
with small boat sheds
graying along a narrow inlet.

Brackish reminders of salt cod
permeate the damp fish house
last filled with a catch
processed over ten years ago.

Brine as hard as quartz
in wooden bins, rotting nets
and barrel stays scrambled
with rusting iron poles
clutter a bleached floor once
slick with blood and sea water.

Two centuries of family ties still
claim this place with names etched
on moldering stones in a cemetery
perched among jagged rocks

overlooking a weathered village
with millions of cod, once
splayed on platforms in the sun
like drying laundry,
shipped out to a world
beyond this shore

where melting icebergs
follow their summer course
and whales breech and dive
through vaulting cerulean waves.

Point Amour Lighthouse

Beacon of concrete and brick
pulsing a path through hidden
rocks beyond jagged shore—

solitary pilot for those astray
in fog and shifting reefs—
guides to safe harbors up the coast.

Bruising waves batter its
moldering groundwork
anchored to granite rock

while sea-wrecked hull
forsaken by fog and man
one moonless night

many tides ago, rusts in salty
ebb and flow that carried sailors
to secret coves and treasure.

Pillar of hope and vision keeper
aged by wind and water
stands alert to dreamers lost at sea.

Lighter Than Air

Our hot air balloon drifted
on primordial wind and fire,
its shadow teasing dingoes
in pursuit over parched Outback.

In good faith that what goes up
will safely come down, we left
earthly concerns below and flew
on whim, untethered and free

above the blush of red rocks
sculpted by time—a desolate
beauty with dried *billabongs*
and aboriginal stone paintings

hidden from aerial view,
all lost in tranquility
broken only by sporadic blasts
of flames taking us higher.

Unexpected Gifts

Lean and elegant with brown
body wrapped in orange
and white printed cloth,

a Masai woman reaches toward
the open window of a public van
where I sit on my way to the Mara River.

She holds a small wire ring entwined
with red and blue beads while motioning
for my left hand to fit her offering.

Kind refusals are lost in the savannah light
and her brilliant smile. It is for me,
this handmade jewelry that requires

a reciprocal gesture of something treasured
in that treeless, spare place. My gift of a
Bic ballpoint pen completes the exchange.

With the brush of our fingers, a pen
and one little ring, two cultures and
eight thousand miles dissolve.

Nippon Memories

1

The doll with pale porcelain face
and thick black hair wears a kimono
woven the color of persimmons,
neatly cinched with yellow sash.

My father brought back other
mementos from Occupied Japan
like the cloisonné jars and lacquered
bowls, ivory *netsukes* and chopsticks
from Kyoto that filled a glass cabinet
in the living room.

He also returned with two warriors'
swords, a military pistol, stories
of beauty and destruction,
sake and blood

in the Land of The Rising Sun
where kamikaze honor and geisha girls
played their roles with a conviction
and grace extinguished in a country
crushed like fallen cherry blossoms.

2

Decades later I travel to Tokyo
where stylish dresses and designer shoes
have replaced silk robe and brocade *obi*,
fluttering fan and wood-soled *geta*.

No longer the charred and mangled city
destroyed by firebombs, sleeping dragons
wake as glass and steel high rises;

compact cars crawl from light
to light, pedestrians pack every inch
of sidewalk, and the bullet train sprints
from town to town.

I drink the warm rice wine,
eat the *kobe* beef with chopsticks
held in place by my right thumb
and between index and middle
fingers the way my dad taught me,
sit shoeless on a straw *tatami*
at a low table where tradition
bows but doesn't surrender.

3

Pink-bottomed monkeys swing
and climb among dense trees
along a narrow road twisting
forty-eight times past stone
cliffs and tiny altars to ancient gods

blessing the route to Nikko,
a montage of Shinto shrines
painted red and verdigris,
their pitched roofs outlined
with carvings of mystic apes
and a sleeping cat.

Beating drums from inside
a sanctuary keep rhythm
to chanting and clapping
white-robed priests, keepers
of centuries-old customs
in this sacred place.

Its solace permeates the hills,
tile roofs, time between time,
contributes more seeds planted
by prayer and ancestry
in the resurrected landscape.

4

In Kyoto I find the old beauty
of prewar Japan with musky
wooden buildings pinched
together on cramped streets

fronting stalls with fresh fish
nestled on glittering ice chips,
costly melons, lemony fruits
and pear-like *nashi.*

I wander through this city
rich with cultural treasures
and imperial history
exempt from bombing,
to look for markets where
my father might have learned
about the art of enamel decorating
or bought my doll now tucked
away in a tissue-lined box.

Perhaps he heard the bee-like
drone of monks with their
nasal *Om*, entered the columned
temple with a thousand and one
carved buddhas—then felt
a rush of forgiveness,
the astonishment of peace.

III

Traveling the World

Listen more carefully to lilt
of voice, passion of clicks
and glottals, smiling words,
the staccato or flow

of any language and hear
hope after the handshake
with a stranger who also
seeks a better world.

Speak more plainly, not
the spew from politicians,
desperate salesmen, sirens'
promise of fairy tales come true.

Embrace the conspiracy of peace
sprinkled among bitter crumbs
of war while fists open
to calls of understanding—

amity beyond frozen hatred,
newly grounded tolerance,
a lost dream awakened
from the darkness of despair.

Walking with a Stranger

It was Mrs. Martin, housemother
of the girls' freshmen dorm,
who told me a young white lady's
reputation and hanging out
with "colored boys" didn't mix.

Her warning was never tested
beyond tennis or chats
in a café where the waitress brought
a Southern Rhodesian classmate
and me cold coffee.

That was the Sixties in Iowa,
when cornfields and churches drew
more attention than Mississippi chaos
dressed in white sheets and police uniforms,
and Midwest small town hospitality
extended to polite greetings.

Two hundred miles east and fifty
years later, I say a quick hello
and walk past a Black man wearing
work gloves to roll himself
in a rickety wheelchair with worn tires
over cracked sidewalks and curbs.

Metallic squeaks and rubber bumping
on concrete follow me until I turn
and look past him, wondering
if I should offer a push up a slow incline
toward city center.

For a moment the choice hinges
on a ghostly voice and old taboos
before we travel over a familiar route
that has changed.

**Women's March,
January 2017**

Once again
I put one step
in front
of the other
forty years later
and this time
with thousands
chanting, roaring
like a wave
ripping
through us,
many led
by those not yet
born when
other marches
demanded
the equal rights
women still claim
on this winter day
with full-throttle sun
glinting off placards,
looming towers,
the nameless faces
who expect
fair pay,
decent healthcare
and equal voice,
with strong resolve
that hereafter
our footsteps

will imprint
a victory
in the pages of history.

At the end of the day, I wedge
onto the crammed train
where a teenage girl stares
at my old ERA button,
then offers me her seat
while she stands the rest
of my way home.

Broadway and Devon

My car idles at a long red light
while city traffic creeps past,
and an old man, bent at forty-five degrees,

clutches two grocery bags dangled close
to the cracked sidewalk where he slides
each foot forward into gnawing west wind.

I sit armored by glass and steel
against cold blasts; the broken stranger
keeps shuffling toward the light.

As we wait for a green signal,
the landscape of our lives
briefly intersects before he blurs

toward obscurity in the rearview mirror
and I, swallowed by rush hour gridlock,
look for the next sign of hope.

CTA

This is the usual run, mostly on time,
mostly uneventful except for the human
landscape of bobbing heads riding
the train south to Chicago stations
downtown or beyond.

No one catches a stranger's eye.
Some stare into books and swaying
newspapers; others talk in garbled
conversations competing with rail
screech or recorded announcement
for the next stop.

A woman bundled in a hooded fleece
jacket, resembling a twelfth-century
monk on a warm April day, bends over
as if in prayer.

At Belmont a young gum-cracking mother
boards with a stroller and sleeping child
who's oblivious to popping pink bubbles
or her mom's bored glances at riders.

Unnoticed, a snoring man slumps
on a cane, his body bulging
between two seats while he grips
a ripped plastic bag.

Another man dressed in white shirt
and crooked tie weaves down the aisle as
he shouts God's praises and offer
of salvation.

It's all here—our stories left unspoken,
small gestures ignored and forgotten,
the smell of mortality before each
of us exits.

Looking Down

Once in a while it's useful to fly
over Kansas and points west.
Greens and browns
paint a landscape puzzle
plentiful in another time

before spiring cityscape
knit together by endless concrete
peppered with parking meters

too small to glimpse
from my cabin window
and too distant to hear

progress bulldozing
the future
far from fresh air

that still blows over
the last prairies and farms
quickly disappearing
through the clouds.

South Road

Late afternoon sun trips
over the mountains, spills
shafts of gold on fall meadows
bordered by tumbled stone walls.

The Whitneys' gray barn
refuses collapse, its stalls empty,
the silo a shell bereft of silage
with domed roof leaking light and rain.

Smoke wisps from the white frame
house standing sentinel
four generations against time,
a few apples still clinging to gnarled trees

like a tickle of longing
for something quieter
before microchips, smart phones
or six-lane highways.

Faded tintypes don't reveal forgotten graves
hidden by underbrush, crop failures,
or the long days into night
farmers wore like tattered overalls.

There is still a history of home that adorns
itself in mute testimony to what's left
sliding and splintering into a place
 that writes its own stories.

The Viewing

We ride beside death,
its dazzling profile
sheathed in a shiny gray hearse,
whitewalls spinning
toward hallowed ground.

In the front sit
two starch-shirted men,
each mute as the rider
oblivious to this last journey
blazoned with tulips and hyacinth.

The radio from our passing car
pounds exploding rhythms
that urge us to speed up,
wave our brightly spun scarves,
thumb our noses
at the poor stiff
who can't hear the music,
feel the titillating vibrations
or cool breeze
rippling our hair.

Instead we mumble our condolences
to no one in particular
and mostly to ourselves.
We slow down and let the pale rider
pass us by.

IV

Back Where I Started

While I can't travel faster
than the speed of light
and journey back in time,

a flip of yellowed calendar
pages reduced to scribbled
memos and names

day by day, year into year
launches memories
of what can't be altered,

what can only be revisited
at best with keener insight
and forgiveness for breaches

of smart choices or joy
for decisions like risking
an unlikely love.

If I could warp space-time,
return to the past, take
different paths,

carry less baggage, would that
alter this day's plans
or the shafts of early light

washing across a new page
holding more or less
second chances?

Taking an Easier Path

For years I raced on cross-country skis
up and down five-hundred-foot hills
with curves, bumps, ice and cold,
bent over thin runners on the descent
and edging herringbone style
to the top.

Stab of poles, plunge, courage
and thrill of conquest melded
at the bottom with flattened
ribbons of icy, sharp turns
through winter's stark beauty.

This February my skis shush
on gritty white, the forest's silence
splintered by a mallard's throaty call
broadcast from unruffled river
below shore while a doe stares
past me toward dipping sun.

No climbs or plummets here
or struggle to compete with nature,
only what comes with boundless
rush of kick and glide blazing
new tracks on fresh snow.

Beach Time

When long-ago bikini fades
into one-piece swimsuit,
a different slant on life
sifts like fine sand
through grasping fingers

and there's no way to swim back
or float for hours in youthful
innocence when radiant tan
and sun-streaked hair
held sway over caution.

It's now when you meet
yourself coming and going
in a watery world of memories,
salty aftertastes mixed
with sunburned longing

for another era when waves
washed hopes and dreams
over you, when the scattered
sea glass, smooth pebbles
and bleached shells

hadn't been collected yet
as reminders of passing time
before yesterday, and more
frothy rollers pound the beach
into tomorrow.

Lesson from the Mountains

Sometimes the path grows steep
and the air slices into thinning doubt
but you keep walking
past bitter stones of hope.

A crescent moon competes
with shimmering sun
that washes over resilient granite
like an urgent call

to unwrap the fortitude saved
for sudden barbed winds
that splinter your heart
like the white bones of dead trees.

Golden flames of light
exhaled by autumn aspens
remind you to crack open
crystals of courage

on your halfway to somewhere,
each bite of translucent sky
big enough to swallow
all fear.

No Ticket Required

Follow the birds, their collage
of changing formations,
their swooping and soaring

as they wing each day
into the next—this moment
the one they know best.

Preparation for nest
or meal requires diligence,
the fortitude to join

the greater whole, the same one
compelling our call and response,
the desire to defy gravity.

Heading West

We don't have to remember
every pink-bottomed cloud,
what catapults or slithers
in our direction

just as waves forget they snarl
into white-lipped rollers
that hurl toward the beach
or softly sweep the shore.

It's in the doing: every inch inhaled,
every mile exhaled,
the impervious sun blazing
farewell to Nebraska corn stubble

stippling farms until spring's greening,
lone red-tailed hawks,
sprawling pastures grazed
by meaty Herefords.

All those treeless towns, weathered cafés
and dusty ranches add up
to people's lives barely glimpsed
from speeding cars with travelers

who can only imagine nineteenth-century
pioneers' heaving wagons
or Pony Express Riders
hell-bent for California.

Remote fields flatten toward
the horizon cradled
by mountains with peaks
lost in clouds and time.

Here, open space unclutters
corners of our lives
packed with trivia that blinds us
to this unrehearsed beauty.

Recalibration

The image I had of myself
wandered among open fields
of fireweed and nesting larks,

blazing sunrise and set, billowing
clouds stretching toward guarantees,
a route perfected by oblique design.

But life's gyroscope reformats
tadpole dreams, demands disjunctive
footsteps with no star charts

for easy passage, as living long enough
reminds me, while I travel
in my time capsule and discard

old brass keys from missing doors,
retrofit corners stuffed with expired
memories and shed boxes of never again.

I start to feel like Kepler unleashed
from old expectations who found
predictable orbits in limitless space.

Navigating Water

1

Breath bends a poem,
a storm loosens rain,
words transmitted by a tower
fold and wash out to sea.

2

A note decomposes to a whisper,
empties and folds like a voice
grown watery with desire –
the music loosened by silence.

3

No satellite or photo finish
to measure the emptiness
when you folded into sky, rain,
a sink churning with falling tears.

4

Streams bend toward a river
emptying into the sea
while each day pumps toward
the watershed of our lives.

5

Fish shapeshift into rivers
of words rising like music
empty of desire, breath
and a sea of tears.

6

Whispering music falls
like water, harnesses the silence,
reminds you that notes inform
an empty refrain.

7

A satellite decomposes your poem
shapeshifting between breath and tears
that speak silent desire – a torn photo
folds and washes out to sea.

8

Harness a river, gather storm
and voice, let the dead fish
of dreams sink like music
without notes. Build a tower.

Traveling Light

All the indispensable maps
and guidebooks have expired,
heavy luggage expelled
to a basement corner
with Grandmother's trunks
from eighty years ago,
and I am left wondering
what might happen
if I were to travel
with only the shirt
on my back and nothing
to burden what's left
of the journey.

ABOUT THE AUTHOR

Susan T. Moss is the author of two books of poetry: *Keep Moving 'til The Music Stops* (Lily Pool/Swamp Press, 2006) and *In From The Dark* (Antrim House, 2014). Her work has appeared in numerous journals, anthologies and magazines, as well as on radio and cable. Susan has served six terms as president of Illinois State Poetry Society. She has been awarded a Vermont Studio Center residency and two Illinois Humanities fellowships. Susan is a graduate of Middlebury College Bread Loaf School of English.

This book is set in Garamond Premier Pro, which had its genesis in 1988 when type-designer Robert Slimbach visited the Plantin-Moretus Museum in Antwerp, Belgium, to study its collection of Claude Garamond's metal punches and typefaces. During the fifteen hundreds, Garamond – a Parisian punch-cutter – produced a refined array of book types that combined an unprecedented degree of balance and elegance, for centuries standing as the pinnacle of beauty and practicality in type-founding. Slimbach has created a new interpretation based on Garamond's designs and on compatible italics cut by Robert Granjon, Garamond's contemporary.

Copies of this book can be ordered
from all bookstores including Amazon
and directly from the author,
Susan T. Moss
609 E. Center Ave.
Lake Bluff, IL 60044.
Please send $18 per book
plus $4.00 shipping in IL
and $6.00 beyond IL
by check payable to
Susan T. Moss.

•

For more information on the work of Susan T. Moss,
visit www.antrimhousebooks.com/authors.html.